Psaltery and Serpentines

a book of poems

by

Cecilia Martínez-Gil

Gival Press

Arlington, Virginia

Published by Gival Press, an imprint of Gival Press, LLC.
For information please write:
Gival Press, LLC, P. O. Box 3812, Arlington, VA 22203.
Website: www.givalpress.com
Email: *givalpress@yahoo.com*
First edition ISBN-13: 978-1-928589-5-25
Library of Congress Control Number: 2010933401
Format and design by Ken Schellenberg.
Cover Design by Ricardo Giordano (Montevideo, Uruguay, 1986).
Photo of Cecilia Martínez-Gil by Jan Vogels.

Advance Praise for *Psaltery and Serpentines*

"*Psaltery and Serpentines* kisses its readers on the mouth so that the poetry becomes 'the ripe fruit to . . . lips,' and one wakes to loving poetry, this poetry in particular. Cecilia Martínez-Gil welcomes the reader into the world of poetry as a partner in the creative act, and readers engage this book-length seduction as tango partners and 'symphonic creatures.' The title poem, the book's first, 'warms this intimate anticipation / with a smile whose mouth dreams of you.' The 'luscious lyrics' of these sweet sounds together could turn 'audiences of statues' into play mates in the affair of Eden. The taut language of each poem is also a sultry music as the book's title promises. By the time one has arrived at the poem 'your language opens the mouth of me' one has taken up residence in the intimate and joyful space of creativity. The rendezvous brings to steady light the ironic match between *lecteur et écrivain:* 'in each one of my spoken silences / you chose me / to ignite me in phosphorus.' Opening this book to any of its poems will sweep the imagination into the poet's creation, and its reviewer's lips will burn for hundreds of kisses."

—Rich Murphy, author of *Voyeur*
and judge for the 2009 Gival Press Poetry Award

"In these sensual poems, language itself is 'a blue garland of desire,' infusing the world with beauty, magic, and sadness. Poetry is 'a temple where prayers become songs.' 'On this stage,' Martínez-Gil writes, 'the ongoing monologue/of a woman's life/has the irresistible hope/born out of her own resilience.' This is a luscious and lustrous collection of poems, a delightful first book from a poet who demonstrates convincingly here both the gravity and the joy of her calling."

—Gail Wronsky, author of *Dying for Beauty*

"Reading Cecilia Martínez-Gil's collection of *psaltery serpentines*, one feels the supremacy of metaphor and music over meaning and sense. Her language is not so much a communication, but rather a melodic carpet ride, a sailing above mundane, loveless, sexless life, a ride that overwhelms sense, that allows one to forget reaching irritably for message in the meaning, so as to be in complete possession of Keats' 'negative capability'—-allowing one to exist inside the seduction of sound, unanticipated metaphors, and the suggestion (hint really) of symbolic objects, to achieve not exactly what the poet means to say, but what the reader needs to hear. In the end, readers feel as if they've been kissed, stroked, seduced and satiated all in one exhilarating reading. From the first day Cecilia walked into my creative writing class this has been her poetic modus operandi, and I count myself fortunate to have mentored her journey, in some small measure, along her chosen path."

—Prof. Mario René Padilla, Santa Monica College

for Federico, sum of love & raison d'être
for Magaluna, muse of life & joie de vivre

Para (y por) mi mamá:

"Because I feel that, in the Heavens above,
The angels, whispering to one another,
Can find, among their burning terms of love,
None so devotional as that of 'Mother'
Edgar Alan Poe

My special gracias to my mentor Mario Padilla, my amazing teacher (who now insists on calling me "colleague"), my dear friend and (it cannot go unsaid) father of my daughter's BFF&E: thank you for teaching me to jump note to note beyond the musical charts of languages.

Acknowledgements:

Thankful acknowledgement is made to the editors of the following publications in which my poems appeared:

Language and Culture (online at languageandculture.net):
   "rites of passages, rites of ashes"

Voices: A Santa Monica Women's College Publication
vol. 3, no. 1/and online:
   "after the ashes"
   "dreams"

Voices: A Santa Monica Women's College Publication
vol. 2, no. 1:
   "pioneers" here as "memories as pioneers of my mouth"

Muecas de Fósforo: Libro de Poemas
(poems originally published in Spanish version)
Ediciones Caballo de Fuego: Montevideo, Uruguay, 1984:
   "childish gestures in a lit match"
   "innocent gestures in a lit match"
   "hands of loves and riots"
   "your habit of untying my ankles"
   "your language opens the mouth of me"

Contents

Psaltery and Serpentines

Son coeur est un luth suspendu;
sitôt qu'on le touche il résonne.
—*de Béranger*

psaltery and serpentines

poised messages pondering
lingered gleams
is this vivacious dance in the air,
letters whose wings are open
to envelope me of promises.

our rendezvous warms this intimate anticipation
with a smile whose mouth dreams of you.
i lick the rim of the envelope
and i glide into the lutes that play these tangible sounds
within this moment.
this is music that flies feathers in the ether
my body will be music today
and i will whisper wind in your ear
from chiming strings.
my lips will come later, smoothing the roads of your ear
riding around the curves of your neck
and returning forever to give you the
thrill that awakens
the absoluteness of song.

i ready you to enjoy
while i rock this delay again
to arrive in you as psaltery,
shaped by three vertices
guiding me to linger my resonances in you,
while you, like a lute, this oud with tense chords
ricochet in repeated resonances of harmonic sounds.

we know how to feel this music
blooming into symphonic creatures,
for i walk to hone these sounds
to bemoan without cost of words.

so at the end
my spirit can unravel the notes
and land on my skin, and leap onto this page
as written, wriggling, writhing words
like serpentines.

pale re-creation

language,
tongue turning inside my mouth
and requiting your savory gibberish.

i inhale your music
to spill it like poems on a silver tray
as i beg you
not to get me naked outdoors.
but you know that the wind will bring
shapes of flames
blazes like tongues.
what you don't know is that this morning too
death passed by
in a loss like blame
killing birds and tossing them in the air
in a pale re-creation of what we could become.

some places in this world are of faded nature
and yet, the water catches fish to give to desperate mouths
so i hunger for languages that speak out
though they speak in tongues,
condemned to regret the wish for a better love
in a recovered world.
for this conceited love makes me speak
inconceivable languages.

dandelions and the wind

wind
makes fretful sounds
like human voices.
wind spilling out breath upon soft wavering meadows
whereas you—entering this region--
become the soundless kiss
blowing the ethereal feathers of dandelions
upon my lips,
and you, as quick as wind, are departed.

gauging the distance,
my arms and legs
are like crossed frontiers,
but you are the one
who flies away like a comet
with a coma of dandelions.

my dandelions are the fragile bakers
blown away from native gardens.
owners of freedom once,
dandelions took along desires
immersed in an invisible sea
and now they float above ground level.

it no longer matters
if this is cause or consequence
of my meager choices
or the true reasoning of my tribulations,
for i only longed to love you beyond ecstasy
while our embrace turned giant windmills.

i summon sadness

El sentido de que no se ha odiado a la vida,
de que se tiene para ella un sentimiento de gratitud,
puede ser el fondo de una obra.

Escritos
Luis Gil Salguero

subterfuge of words
depending upon an answer to make sense,
is equal to just sinking in sadness.
i come to trickle on this table this sadness of today
hence, you can see this
deformed creature that our love has become.

my anger is mutating into misery
and i watch it squeaking over the table.
i too, sink in gray ashes of other people's nostalgias
and carry within their irreversible questions
like bubbles blown by dreams
but burst by desire.

fullness means nothing else
except a green field of sunflowers
where brightness could be touched
as i used to touch your aura
and as you used to sense the light shed
so wholly over my skin.

so evolved we were
as it was the air conquering,
and courting our world of
togetherness.
for we were free,
we had
permission to breathe.

then, men came riding horses
and their horses trembled by the gateless fences
the cavalry sounded like drums
storming upon the ground,
awakening an array of emotions
making of my today a sad hum…
all over me i could feel their spears
spiraling through my skin
like arrowheads bitten by bullets.

but distance is a spot of brittle sadness
summoned to arrive
in the fencing laws of anxiety.
the sleeplessness of my voice goes then to perspire,
as an illustrious aid
to shut the shout that i must utterly mutter.

and as i walk the stairs and walk away
i transmute
i transcend into a ravine——transformed in a confused path--
i too blend the two worlds from my own transition:
woman and man made of coal and salt,
womb
man wooing woman.

so the night leaves me fainting
by the thin borders of a formless river
subtly digressing,
sinking into the profile of new night.

mulberry fingers

he was mouth watering
i wanted to be poured into him
but he was hot
mordacious
bold,
while the inclemency of the weather painted
of mulberry
my fingers.

after that shivering cold that he too dribbled over me
i painted nevertheless,
drawing in the air
as if, truly!
i was to draw more than just incongruent lines;
but my mulberry fingers could,
they were the ones drawing up lines on a steamed glass
and the lines drawn up by my mulberry fingers
had movement
and they were possible, they were figures
who had lives of their own
they had fullness and persona.
and were so humid these drawings upon the air
that one day they went away
for only dreamt of becoming
Chinese shadows featuring at The Magic Lantern.

in the wolf's mouth

hermit trains transporting full luggage
of ballads and *milongas* of the fields
played by lonely guitarists
whose only audience is a dimming sun.
at night the station is hidden,
and tonight, the train station is a dark wolf's mouth,
where—luckily--
one can only distinguish non human steps.
even so,
he arrives by air in a land of never.

at sunrise
there will be no place for me at his porch
where he usually plays his banjo.

in the meantime, i will stay in this middle-of-the-night
for it feels safe here in this wolf's mouth:
i slumber in its lukewarm tongue
and smell his desire for sweet blood.

today, i no longer fear the loner trains,
and everything is so small that fits into my hand
as i stretch my arm to reach the remote control
and turn it on (or off?)

era de tango

quick sighting to enter your realm
like a running deer
who dares to tip over your breath upon all possible endings.
i come to make myself as woman
pouring from my lips
nothing but stories and sounds
of an abandoned *bandoneón*
while your psaltery creates this:
our era of tango.

our bodies are boundless beings
dancing on the ground in rebellion
and crumbling into waves of an indescribable sea
as we tango on the immaculate tile
you in black tuxedo and sleek hair,
me a Scarlet from a farther south.
until my skirt claims your bowtie
unfurling you in shades of red,
as if it were possible
love between deer and deer hunter.

yet,
it is happening, this sudden transformation,
so i tango tears of cravings
for we have the visa to befit, besiege the frontiers
while this dance lasts.

taboo kisses

underneath his tuxedo's lapels he has tenderness.
with his fingers, he lifts them up
and--magician man--
he releases butterflies fluttering upon his chest
and nectaring into my belly button.

but yesterday, from the ocean
i could see distance from a wise perspective
and as i paddled the pillows i saw concealed kisses
afraid to be caught like fish in a marine net.

for these kisses can become
taboo kisses that adulterate the blood
and threaten to poison hope,
although you may not die
nor want to die in the sweetness of this bliss
a little every day,
even though you have no idea
that there will be, still, more pain.

mantle of fear

that one (and first) time
there were subtle mysteries
enticing the lovers to altars with strewn flowers,
spread of petals.
they worshiped each other
until the candles melted away.

but the man-lover was personifying a fear
refusing to unveil his lover's eye
because the sun and the fire were,
suddenly, a machine gun of rays
smoking the wax as gun powder,
of burning candles,
inviting to smolder the smelling mist
that cloaked them within, but without warmth.
thus, sadness was this chameleonic mantle of fear
and he was leaning by her left side
stitching her wounded elbows.

another time pagan Eros invited the lovers to think,
about dying for love,
but the woman would die not.
instead she asked Eros to leave,
she said
--i seek a life that'd fit the size of my cupped hands.
so Eros left, and she danced the transparency
of a life that filled the insides of her hands,
while her lover's fingers could play stringed music,
music that her body danced
as she smiled a small smile.

like stars once guided the pilgrims of lovers' dreams
books guided me to search and to find.

i too sought the tangible territory
of my impossible lover
sought to fist it, fit it.
but this one has left too
unfurling and sprawling serpentines
without celebration.

but i endured like a lasting prayer's light
so i tossed aside the mantle of fear.
and i danced the clarity of my night
and i smiled
surely, an immense smile.

a sunset left behind

while getting naked
through his playing fingers
distant sheets of beliefs
aim geographically to dictate
the turns of my extended body,
until i become skin and skin becomes this sheet
a skin of seamless fabric
with dunes that afar seem as liquid as seas.
but then, these seas begin to surround me:
they make me an island,
an isolated island where only lonely boats
could be marooned
and i am marooned too, when his fingers play no more.

like these lonely boats, i am.
we come to doom ourselves to a fervor
until we are futilely forgotten
thus, we leave,
leave like the ocean waters leave behind
a red-ballooned sunset.

chamber of melted sounds

fruits fallen in cotton sheets,
our affair--
mingled with these frequent silences,
rhythmically connected to Miles Davis's trumpet sounds.
as sacred as the air,
sublime sounds bestow a generous identity
to this nameless love,
so i write this poem
that helps me to become the ripe fruit to your lips
and the free bird to my soul.

hence i fly, and this poem remains
at the mercy of the wind
'till i return, again
graceful and captivated to chisel your face
pour life in your mouth to make it shudder with indulgence.

soon after,
i render a thought of forgiveness to your selfishness
carved in sounds furrowing our skin into this pleasure,
circumnavigating the world in this precious instant
that lets us plunge
like ghosts
upon ripe fruits as if they were feathers:
our buoyant bodies rising and falling
'round the timely sounds of Miles Davis.

a shadow pinned to his winter coat

it was May, the midst of the south's autumn.
she was blonde,
looming across the river.
he moved like a pendulum
and i, had been already composed as music.
the three of us, serendipitously
crisscrossing the southern hemisphere's winter
extending its origins into a puzzled September
just about the time when Montevideo's train station
was going to become remembrance
before time.

these tickets are a way to slide names inside our pockets
and to say goodbye to shadows
utterly pinned to a saxophone case.

the musician stretched the tides
and surfed through the nights
until it was morning
and he would come to my doorstep
to feed me breakfast.
i stayed
but my shadow walked away looking back
to show me that i was pinned to his winter coat.

crossing my seasons
it was me sometimes——or was it my shadow?——
who loved him until dawn
and disintegrated autumn leaves each morning
from the darkest blue 'till the breath of spring,
the south's eve of September.

yet, he climbed these seasons
as a summer's *tour de force*,
while i drenched in my own heavens
and i spared more than a few crows
inventing a temple where prayers became songs
lasting many more Septembers.
unlike us.

Montevideo's mouth

is mute
a city that does not speak unless it does
at winds' will
so i won't forget this one feeling of loving her.

i bury the misfortune of my--constantly--
going nowhere
leaving zero tenants to inhabit my dwellings.
meantime,
i have left already,
left behind my solitary hours
the growing shadow in my face,
for i know my kisses will scratch her skin
and keep her away from suggesting that she also
wishes to stay
tonight.

yet, i remain to give her a voice
by the hour with this timeless clock
like a bastard punching his id card.

but i,
i make love by the halves and taste her breasts,
this, her
subtle love that will appear in his perfume
and will vanish in my skin…
or so i wish to believe-- .

when she is ready to escape through the window,
even after the breath of her spell
still remains bathing my skin,
my life of subtitles and stereotypes
will estimate the inks of stripping her
of my inexact memory
while i am smuggling my papers on this amused error
so inevitably getting away
like some do,
for my memory serves me right.

duendes and *despertares*

who looks outside, dreams;
who looks inside, awakes.
Carl Jung

nights are pending
and i roll upwards in a world of vice versa
to which, obviously, i do not belong.
you are standing before me and behind the window
so i finger-paint the silhouette of your legs
in a chessboard-like sky.

the full night has awaken *duendes*
who dance between the moonlight and me.
like a *duende* who transcends the real world
i am inhabitant of my dreams
who once escaped from the beginnings
of a life as wandering boat, until you asked of me
to become your lighthouse
to be the safe haven.
each time that the storm unraveled inside
i was the tower whose light fed us of radiance,
the beam that gave us direction.

but,
i know too
that
my dream condemns you to darkness
while i reverse my odyssey
and (as boat again) guided by a single star
i voyage within.

stapled lemon, stapled honey

ants crawl my skin
tartar flavor dominate the vista of this lime-like afternoon
bitter tongue looks for a dream
inside any given thirsty mouth of voices . . . sour swish

stapled honey stapled lemon
he walks by
zesty honey skin
lemon trunks
indeed i am delaying the night
between hopes and mirrors
for i have omens fearing to become dissolved pieces
in my mouth,
or dreading to bleed the loneliness
contained in my body
and mess up this emerald ocean.

afternoon spilled from a dream
i flee with a stranger
because i know how to blind-fly.
as the twilight falls on the sand
thoughts are like broken shells
and no one risks becoming pieces on a single afternoon
if there is enough light to cast passion.

> ...love would never leave us alone,
> against the darkness there must come out the light.
> could you be loved... and be loved...
> Bob Marley

before fading to black

the horizon carries
devastating clouds
overwhelmingly squashing the sun.
these shadows seize the city
and arrive at my feet
like letters that were never sent.

i can see my home through this window
a house full of your belongings,
(those that you used share with her),
and nothing claims me
except my imaginary flavor of you.
i cannot reach you
not even from the garden,
for my hands are as adamant
as roots
hidden below the ground
pulling me, keeping me earthbound.

i can see that she walks in and smells your presence
as a wolverine would smell the blood
of your darkest night with me.
she does not howl
not even in her trespass.
instead, she cries
(i can see everything from the other side of the glass)
she gloves my handkerchief
wanting to disguise her weeping hand.
she kisses it and before fading to black
i can tell that she too had been in love.

ocean water in a paper cup

woven afternoon
afternoon of threads launched in the horizon.
threads of light swinging
hanging from the air
as if sweet marionettes were playing on this stage
that is this vast ocean
illuminated by predominant violets and purples
still shining on this quiet beach.

message in a bottle:
we are sand and salt
we were pirates of irretrievable boats
and do not get to be
rescued by this light.

thus, we cry for this spectacle of the afternoon
of violet and purple threads,
we shed tears offering no survival to this romance
even though we marvel at nature's thespian performance.
we are an audience of statues of almost dried nothingness
and our tears too, swing and fall,
not in the sea
but into a paper cup.

unbroken drum skins

eager blood, has the rhythm of *candombe* music
tightening itself in time
while drizzle travels down my skin
to heal a wound between my breasts.
yet, the dagger sinks below the flap
and the heart is as open flesh beating at *candombe* clave
bare hand, hand with stick
slap and tap tap

the hands of my black people bled
before their fingers hardened
to hit the drum-skins of the *candombe* congas.
i dance a trance that takes me away from disillusion
and the skins of their drums break the masks
before their hands can scar.
slap tap-tap, *chico repique piano* drums
tambor piano like a hammering tenor
a black musician hitting the bare hide with his raw hands.

this cruel afternoon full of plums
fills me of impatience:
i am an ungrateful drum
because i scar.

lusting love

we are here
ignoring evolution
petal and ivory made flesh
we are the origin of the world.

you continue to be the axis of my nights
as you make them succulent
while ravishing me out of a fragile darkness.
what a volcano this one night!
and all its summit is iridescent, incandescent
an instant of pure light
where there is more than the fleeting certainty
of a lusting love

blue-penciled by the seashore

man ocean
makes this woman of sand,
she lies stretching along the borders of the world
longing for the sultry touch
drenched in warm sun,
woman of sand,
woman of eroded particles of earth
flushed down by rivers,
crystalline sand is the subliming sum of her existence.
in the ebb and flow
she reaches out
but man of ocean cannot be held.

he is of water,
thus, he riddles down through sandy pores
escaping her fingertips:

> *nothing in his nature is graspable*
> *only his smell,*
> *marine layer*
> *lingering in the air*

woman of sand christened by the sea,
man of ocean
hazel-ing the horizon where the sea births waves.
he rolls wild upon her
wooing her without aim.

ocean man is like a veiled surprise, curled within the spume.
he is in motion
ever-changing inside a cocoon.
man of ocean unsettled in its splendid metamorphoses,
restless in his serene gaze, he smiles Mona Lisa
while she becomes a Marc Chagall woman
floating in the perennial loves of her life
and thus, she vanishes:

> *in the elements of art, i give shape to my reason*
> *i bury the spontaneous idea of the kiss*
> *the thirst for the subtle touch*
> *while i paradox in liberty.*

spheres in motion
spheres of desire
clashing waves upon the stillness of this lake
these waves are the enemy of my guarded wants
for the ocean navigates me inside
and i am thirsty of salt water.

these are realms inhabited by the impossibilities
yet, at the beach
when the air is blistered in peace
and warmth is of breezed words,
unrealizable truths become tangible
and i feed off my quivering hands
stirring words upon this passion
so i can unchain me only here, within this poem
as though these words, written on the sand
waited to hear the hard shells breaking, revealing me anew
in the center of whirlpool forces,
for this poem will remain,
blue-penciled by the shore…

but, ah! such realm i inhabit today
i close my eyes: sun basking woman of sand
i whisper myself into the forest of my mind:
in my forest i see fluttering butterflies
and i feel them grazing the borders of my existence
and i,
i let them in!
even for the grace of this unbendable instant
i let them flicker in me, indeed!
i let its wings tempt the boundaries of the forbidden
waves like kisses ebbing in sand
raspberry tongue sweeping my sand castles
whistling ethereal
gusting its eternal mineral
for under this sunlight i am of glistening prisms
skipping at the seashore.

just me, today, woman in sand
immersed in the living elements that erode me
sand-tanned in the poise of the sun,
thrusting rhythm of ebbs and flows.
your gaze grazing my gaze grazing your gaze

alerting alchemy, asking me to craft
words like maps to the impossible.
while it is true that the sea carves the beach
to dwell its array of desires
upon bronzed substances.

> swallow this poem instead of me!

Foucault guides my reason: desire regulates my mouth.
instead
i say *chrysalis*

i taste this word, nibble and chew it,
roll it up in my ethnic drawl…
and before i swallow it, i let it rest on my tongue
i relish this word only to sigh and to moan,
pristine, intangible instant
when onomatopoeias of seduction
become words feasting inside the mouth.

> *in the impetus of waves clashing*
> *i built a dam*
> *a poem that harbors me*
> *in the perennial lighthouse*
> *of my chosen existence*

dreams

once upon a time
there was no wind
the air felt like motionless life
and gravity was a theory based on danceless leaves
falling on the streets of lost cities.

yesterday, i kissed my dream
dancing to bestow a soul into my white dress
while the tolls of my bell-shaped skirt
created the wind to brush my feathered arms.
yesterday, i did not fall,
if only yesterday had stayed just a few more hours,
i wouldn't have fallen today,
and tomorrow would be the shelter,
the promising realm
illuminated by the beam of a lighthouse.

midnight of silence and dim lights surprise me
sleepless and bruised,
the moon had spanned up from the sea
to hide behind the clouds,
showing the restless dance of Earth around the sun.
the sky seemed a never-ending darkness with clever
brilliances fluttering in the air.

i fell asleep,
a walking Alice conceiving a porcelain doll
seeking an unthinkable realm
searching for the breeder of unflawed dreams.
the kiss awaiting me as upshot of substances,
cause i know about the hope of my drifted navigator
who reaches to read the creeds written on the sky.

dawn

'till dawn
in the middle of nowhere
a dawn hanging
its strange orange moon in the sky.

the telephone booth becomes a jukebox
and i listen to the songs of the sixties,
deferred to this morning.
the table turns and turns
and my body is the record,
an opal vinyl
willed by your index finger

--objection your honor
--motion denied

this is an idea of my heart
and it has been useless.
as i evince you wrong, again,
the telephone rings its fourth scream
and i refuse to answer
because i do not want to see the lie
bare under the morning.

i grovel
and you do remain at dawn instead,
for you know that i am the voice that will awake
its own sunrise,
you know that it is not darkness
responding to that possible morning.

tonight, right after twilight,
i will dream about tomorrow
i will replace sorrow with whatever i design
and i will replace me
with a goddess,
the one that will wake up
and see a morning of certainties.

drumming with its fingers
niggling through the window shades,
the sunlight will come to land on your forehead
and i will hold your temples
to prolong the kiss until is not a goodbye any longer.

across the bed
the shadows will stretch until they vanish
and the mirror will show a new wish
like water tendering my skin
wet in the unprivileges of lost pleasures:
for fruits and miracles taste alike
just when the orange moon
is the morning that i create,
even if i must linger out of your love.

let it be a rose in my hands

stop the time
because one more minute without love
and i will mislay you irreversibly.

this instant could be the rare fruit
an anew and renewed exact time,
one that holds this beauty
so justly, inside my hands.
come, so you can squeeze it
come and drink its exquisite juice
for orange drops are thus, juicy words of reconciliation.

lover of this night
be my lover too,
let me have this fruit inside my hand
let it become a rose
let the petals soften my jagged palms
heal the scars, wash the blood,
merge us in remedial union.

this time could be the forgotten ritual of sensual nature
and bring forth the purity of nurturing fruits
even when is almost late to believe its *possibleness*.

the world in my eyes

the world unfolds
but in its garments reveals itself
like an enamored sovereign
of watchful eyes over its kingdom.

my braids down toward my feet.
i turn upside down to hang them from
imaginary branches to make my body swing
like a child, rocking back and forth in the air
feet ungrounded, trees waddling upside down
allowing me to dream a sky
as if it were a blue garland of desire.

back in the city, i decide that i can invent street lamps
coveted in my pupils
to brighten this world,
at the same time as i await for the return of the day,
after that long and prolonged night.
so i pack the remains
of this enduring gaze
and learn to survive even in the city.

i am a still a night watcher
rare owl of crossed eyes
constructing shapes in the shadows
like limbs expanding above
reaching to seize imagined shades of blues,
in order to cease the night, once and for all.

therein, i become passage between the blues
and other gray threats
that once painted
the breath of our nights
and i reach out for new yellows.

but a darkest blue effuses its perfume over me
and i distinguish a king whispering remedies
against ill-fated eyes.
his sovereign affection embraces us,
sublimating this night:
magician musician, knight and ruler,
defiant of overwrought colors of indigoes
that for so many nights have been blistering me.
he sees my eyes and in them their nature,
flowers in a blurry sky of doubled ether,
yellows starry and vangoghians
blossoming as in a blue meadow,
gleaming their enciphering petals
of constantly humid,
restless sparks of a blue vault!

and the night vanishes,
banish its own darkness
leaving the flowers of the sky in my hands
like spilled ink of a poem on canvas
a quest to run through my veins:
for this light comes through illumination
to cast free, autonomous eyes
suiting its natural environment
within.

lexis of emotions

i have a poem wrapped around my tongue.
wet vowel, vacillating consonant
drapery of words that come to
exist through me, today.

my
mother tongue is not my language
for my native voice
is the poetic texture of my being.
tied in a knot i must write
to unravel my essence outwardly,
for there is a force that binds me to my origins
a thread of tears, drop by drop
like footprints staining the soil
with echoes of laughter and sequences of sorrows.

but now,
a delectable
edible vocabulary
envelops me in ephemeral sounds
gasped and whispered,
mumbled and sang,
--most certainly sang--
poetry of luscious lyrics,
delicious writings
a dish of voices multiplying
so there is no more agony, no more grief,
only my living tongue
in the birth of words departing from the center
of its slippery humidity
such a womb this mouth!
for i must reveal these,
my own prophecies,
marry the word to the myth
as the word is pronounced
plummeting within the story.

for all i wish is to speak
lexis of emotions.

sunrays and dust

it is the beginning of a poem
where, like in torrents of lava,
words bleed
running down
to the vast liquid realm of words.

once the words arrive here
in this realm,
they just embrace the might of language:
for words speak for themselves.

each time,
perhaps imagination invents
an evocable vocal
of undeleted words
leaping, limping,
stuttering in its own syllables
calling to mind the consequence
of this stubborn desire of seeking poetry
inside one's own hands.

the beginning of a poem
it is a given
a gift
for the poem just notices this dust on the shelves
dancing in the air
and its seizes its *Devenir*
beyond this minute
an instant enhanced by the beauty
of these afternoon sunrays
warming up one's knee and transforming this idea
into a dimensional door
into the surprise of a smile
like a slap to the heart when it wants to stop beating.
this is the gift: a shoplifting of experiences
opening the gates to new dimensions.
hence, the woman crosses the threshold
and becomes a poet.

dynamics of universe

he is my nationhood
the warm distances between my vertices,
he balances my eco system, the so-called poles of my being.
he is the actual in flowering
of an enthralling crepuscular nap
and thus he watches over me.

he is the achievement of my imperfections,
for i am from a flawed world of vanities,
a woman of tormented mirrors
who walks a path and seizes a torch
guided by his enlightening of me.

my beloved
his green eyes are the algae of my world,
his mercy touches the mugginess of earth
and that's enough to blossom, to moan in harvests
to squeeze life out of a seed
even when the heart is like a fist
and wrestles restlessly,
regretting to dwell in the transparencies of his offerings.

I remember that he came one afternoon that was turning black night
when i wanted to submerge my eyes and forget,
submerge me into oblivion.

yet
he saved me once
he saved me twice
he saved me again
he still saves me.
savior man
savory his cure.

i love him
and this is the verge of my own life
for i knew we were on a godless earth,
first woman first man
wandering upon unknown lands
and stumbling upon remote paradises
of each beginnings of all our lives.

i wink and he smiles
but
who dares to affirm that eleven is the sum of five and six,
or seven and four?
who is bold enough to defy my math?
numbers are projectiles in the back of the neck
as the memories interlace within their own stories
and numbers are just the order of the pages we write,
where i ink and print our love
where he composes our soundtrack,
songs that we are now saving in our pockets
--for when we are old and count back
and tell our tales.

it will be good to know that we saved these songs
for one moment to come, and indeed, it will come.
we know that, then, we will have grandchildren
running about barefoot
with muddy sand glued to their ankles.
grandchildren of coppered hearts tanned nevertheless,
in the twilight of our summer.

blades and gems like thunders

the message of crude words
you screamed
landed on the solid grounds of my conscious will
as a song cried out by Janis Joplin.

yesterday, when the light was wet and slippery
like our bodies in it,
i was still rolling,
escaping the blades of your sharp tongue
while i gave you nothing by gems like thunders
thrown at you in a melancholic reproach.

after i dreamt these reveries of this other mind i carry
you mentioned that the word of honor
would have
the impact of forgiveness against
lightning bolts
clashing on the bare ground of this abode.
but i can't help it but to mind
this madness
and yes i choose
my rain over your thunders
for you don't know i don't ever carry an umbrella.

memories as pioneers of your mouth

Not till they have turned to blood within us,
…no longer to be distinguished from ourselves—not till then
…the first word of a verse arises and goes forth from them.
Rainer Maria Rilke

this way of tasting life
such as today
the idea of the soul deeming into an outrageous love.
fear has gone away
and there were no farewells
or parting revelries.
for i would not miss a day with fear.

but fear was the lonely heart ashamed and hidden
behind its shielded comfort,
fear was the cobweb
immerse in its glumly loathing,
and i pitied
such gloomy doom.

but do not allude to the matters of this silence
for so pervasively this silence persists in my heart
and permeates its throbbing.
and now, it is known,
compassion is truth
and for truth i will thus speak.

my mouth speaks of dreamed kisses
for memories are pioneers of my mouth
and i have always known
that i could not die with their affections.

yet,
i awake encircled by gentle animas
portrayed from my lover's soul
noshing in ciphered potions
lurking to clasp the moment
when i do not have to explain any longer
that i exist
bare and essentially untamed
alive and relieved by memories
aside from the façade
of my life
and its bonfire of forgettable fears and quandaries.

rites of passages, rites of ashes

death be silenced:
so hush to the stillness of the night
sublime in its rhythmical ebb and flow,
and dance at the beach
for this beach, is the retreat from the battlefields.

rush into the arms of your lover
to hear of other rites of tides
hurled from whispering voices
and fostered by gentle claps.

feel the sand, take your sandals off
and commence the dancing around the fire.
let the wolf of the night howl its melancholy to the moon,
let the snake of paradise find its rat
and let it bite it
and devour it until the firing rite of cremation
summons them up from your dance.

this night has been all over her already,
and again, she escapes the ceremony.
she lies down but still dances to clouds of confusion,
interrupters of a flowing rain
that shatters on the surface of the sea,
giving immunity to the fire.

then, after the silence is shushed again
one can hear the waters kissing,
drenched in themselves
while i still watch her dancing
my own rite.

after the ashes

cierro los ojos
oigo en mi cráneo
los pasos de mi sangre
            Octavio Paz

an unusual fire invited me
on the morning of my birthday
to submerge my grief into its wealth of blazes.

i walked emptied and worthless
into its febrile wholeness
the threads of my skin
crumbing the ashes i began to become
swollen unevenly over dealt cards of death
wild cards of life.

after yanking one of her feathers
my goddess swept me
into a circle outlined by her beak.
and curled up on the very ashes i was,
my goddess chanting
hatching,
warming up the myriad hues of gray of my remains.

harassing winds wheedled my goddess,
and sought to blow her away,
or lured her into going
away
and when the rain assaulted her
she unfurled her wings
turning into an umbrella
while i began to link
dry powder to pebbles,
to gravel
to rock,
Earth.

then,
the heat started to diffuse from the ground up,
intense warmth of sharp arrows as blazes,
soaring from the sky
heat in the drops of sweat
sliding from the temples of working men and women,
raw heat of lovers jolting their bodies and their beds,
steaming heat from boiling pots in the kitchens.
heat with and without fire
heat with sparkles ignited by the stars,
dazzling dust inspiring to become
living warmth
thirsty warmth
voracious warmth
awakening heat
awakening
me.

unfair treaty

between us
there is a glass wall:
this dividing bridge of the airports
like a stage for my battle, and your war

two days before
i took a bite of a forbidden fruit,
(the one you've left on my night table,
when later you parted),
and i slept through the morning
chewing sandy feelings,
swallowing the juice of our affair.

fugitive of winged hair
you flew right before madness
could arrive to join us.

you, feeble warrior
disheartening my shield
and i artless
sleeping through your departure.

but i slept,
and i dreamt the oak leaves
that you've rained on me: falling leaves,
undrying me in its withered browns
crunching in their fall
its random autumnness,
so i stepped on them and danced upon their pulsations.

at midnight
when the spell was broken,
i ran and fell too
i, a porcelain vase crashing into pieces,
cruelly landing on the ground
scattering my limbs:
a ground tainted with flowers.

in the following night
once again, i dreamt your lips taunting me
saying goodbye,
pressing against the glass wall
your lips reaching out for the yet unforgotten kiss
that you would later leave
(like a mangled towel)
on my night table.

not an easy task
to ease
to wring
to yield
to cease the loving
two days for truce:
a treaty for a sunset without sun.

light water

on your quest to lightness,
your eyes seemed to carry me
taking me to places where i have never been.
i went through the night
as if the night were a river
where i could wash out grief.

later, in the morning
you soaked me with your thirst
and i with my fluvial futileness,
as we toured this wetland of us.

i crossed against my curse
i crossed my legs,
those legs that i used to use to walk
but i, nevertheless, walked and dared to walk out.

there was a bird in the well of these moors,
drinking water
then, licking its feathers,
earnestly bathing in airiness
and light.
i watched until the conclusion of its chore
at twilight
as i remained regretful,
living my own destiny
immersed in heavy wetlands,
needing your eyes and my gaze.

later, at morning time
torn apart, faithful as light to water
i broke the spell
i walked back
as my curse vanished:
it was a blessing converting
to love.

utter vitality

her wicked hands were planning the touch
to give me grievance
and i knew it was coming.

swiftly,
i felt into despair
thinning out my sibling tears on my pillow,
stroking the sheets in a motherly cuddle:
my breast is my consciousness
feeding place and light
in a new correlation of time and space
thus, i must write

like this poem, i too penetrate this page
reaping and not raping,
we are loving us
as if bodies in motion
were finally conditioned to shape-shift into lullabies.

i feel alive
you feel alive
so suddenly.
but this way, we both can rethink the undone
awake the undead
unbury our remains,
jiggle with our senses
and finally, sort out
the air, the fire, the water and the land,
evenly,
in the wholeness of our bodies.

just dusk

the giant trees spoke to me without words.
immense in the forest
their arms rose to the sky
reaching for what i cannot.

i touch the air, blindfolded
in a game of resistance
dwelling in desires
where i want your voice
your touch, your imagination.

i seek the renewing kiss
the healing word
the thrashing of my desperation.

i am lonely,
scared of the night that you denied me.

your life shielded behind sheer confusion
my last kiss has not been relinquished
and i hope
that today will be the day in which i recover what i´ve lost.

give me the magic of a smile glistening in the early dawn:
return to me
fresh in water
like if nothing
like if darkness would not have taken part in our days.

just dusk.
a glimpse of what cannot be but rather *is*.

remote passages of discoveries within,
like unrequited love,
and you, restless,
to embrace me in renewed passions.

dare
come to me
as if nothing would have darkened you.

giving

give me the path to ease the itching in my throat
that is no more than a desire for feeling a love
and swallow the urgent words of a passion

look at this night from within
and you will see the moon
from our lunar site.

this moon is unique in my world
for i have awaken dormant mirrors
and now they just shine
and shine again
until you can dance and dance
with magical wings
and i receive this courage
granted by your restless imagination.

we are of bodies inventing new fables
myths of us
that once we dreamed of.

just wait
and conceal your heart
so it can see
but not be seen
so
very
open

memory of oranges

because i have foot-printed the load of being
solitary soil,
and in each text the memory awakes,
an orange
opened in the open mouth
seducing the skin
to be a moonlighted syndrome of recoveries
as it splashes behind the bite.

today, the axiom of you is me:
we are the subjects vital to each other's existence,
and i refrain from burning memories
in our fire,
refusing the burning of these papers that i fail to write
because i'd rather love you
and choose to pour in us memories of liquid orange,
running down our throats, after its tender pulp
tingles and tickles our tongues
making us smile its juicy and sunny breath.

grateful for this thirst
for i have been an ingrate,
ill-timed in the anger that sought to burn
our goodbye kisses.

but i now blow you a new kiss, either way,
steeped in orange
and i mingle with a parade of men and women
in the streets of New Orleans,
drunken in coyness:
they teach me to shout the cries of strangling endings.
to set free old choked sounds, out in the alley.

and thus i keep nothing but the flavor
of sweet memories of oranges.

because words can embark too in all tongues,
and travel mouth to mouth
word for word
in word of mouth:
an orange bite able to splash
within the mouths of all centuries.

en la escala de sol

i cannot know of your body
because there is a faulty return

your absence is now
the sleeplessness glitch
of my unsatisfied truths

with my desire
i have attained
the yearnings for a new morning

and i hold on to the fuchsias of the evening
tolling like bells
in this old house of worship.

but i!
i just miss your breath!
your fingers playing with my hair strands
as if they were strings of an instrument,
for you always know
how to compose
musical notes
from the charts of my body:
whole notes
half notes
quarter notes
eighth notes
en la escala de sol
g major scale

si la sol
si la sol
do si la

re re re re re
all you need is love
re re #re #re mi, si
love is all you need

raspberry tongue

i have only
my mind
embedding seeds
that will not flourish

i see you blossoming
on the mane of a man

the sea has an opposite coast
where a lover awaits you without his consent

i discovered your path
and you refused to walk it.
i gave you a map, with hints and choices,
defeaters of the echoes of your unblessed childhood.

here and there,
there are only remains of our one kiss.
your kiss stays in me
your raspberry tongue
is the only fruit that your voice sputtered
grazing across my lips.

i was a clay doll
left to blaze in confusion
while
only from the shelves of your imagination
you remodeled your condition of man.

my seedless mind
expects the rain
that may or may not come.
either way
you are gone
gone to your own orchards of raspberry trees.

gone toward another kiss
and it will be his now,
your raspberry tongue.

harvesting hope

on this stage
the ongoing monologue
of a woman's life
has the irresistible hope
born out of her own resilience.

trenched in grief
she spent her days, a few years
clutching her own jaws in the absence of her mother,
for death is still around
but not luring her to his love.

these thoughts
she achieves without magic,
but as she clings to the Black Orpheus of this poem
i expand my borders
omnipresent in her story
i move away from the margins of his canvas
and i
i soar the blue ethers
every time that in a poem
i harvest her hope.

a new obsession to keep me craving

today
i will you to come
to visit me even if you are a ghost

i want to feel your inescapable presence
trickling down through the light,
conquering the chambers of my isolation.

i am not alone now,
your fingers graze the skin of my forehead
and there are wind chimes
reminding me of your much longed hum.

you are my garden's humming bird,
and if i close my eyes
you tell me that my eyelashes are glowing
in dew, instead.

if i yawn
you cuddle me away from boredom,
you embrace me from the storm
in the tattered receiving blanket of my memories of you.

and if the storm breaks into these quarters
still you advice to scare it away, with compassion.

i will seek a new memory
change the meaning of grief to mean just twilight,
a concept engendering a new obsession
to keep me craving
for you said that i am staying alive.

childish gestures in a lit match

once upon a time
in a castle's abode
he was all body
and if he should let his hair grow
it would caress my shoulders
my bosom it would graze,
and everything would be like trial
or talisman:
like a childish gesture of a lit match
and i'd do nothing
just
watch

i would observe its searing top
sizzling in its tiny fire, crackling in whispers
fizzing and hissing...
still mighty in its minuscule existence,
a miniature torch
even now
so revealing in its humbleness.

it would be right to remain here,
in this small world, to be poetry's favor
indulging in the splendor of words,
a trial to dwell in the gestures of this flame
flickering its reflections on your face
of quivering shadows and lights,
and thus, travel to the past
cleaving to the primal warmth
of a talisman.

innocent gestures in a lit match

time is a thief of itself
one who crawls unscrupulously
in the attics
of my mind,
where some body is locked in
to discover new poems
inventing the fever to feed in itself
his poetic vocation.

but should i were not to remain
looking at these gestures,
it would yield my time
into bridges
and i would ride across on my own,
stealing your silenced consonants
your slept vowels,
and i would let them
cry in the streets
writing themselves on the walls
like protests shaking these bricks
exhaling huffs and puffs that would tear down
your towers.

there is so much to bestow
from one self
that it would be impossible
to accuse me and rather allow the consequences
to follow their own course,
and burn, finally burn those towers
with the unfussy phosphorus of this match.

hands of loves and riots

strange your sonnet
a poem
that i keep discovering.
ironic scene though,
a stage of war designed out of lyrics:
it does resemble your loving
and my country at war.

my essential musk's trance
my journey to write, pirated,
a coup d'état
organized by their hands,
while our hands chose the loving.

five hours of hands
dialoguing with a time of ours.
mutiny of hands,
hands that made love
and made it out of peace and riots.
such luck the luck of these hands!
embracing a trance like musk
incense of musk and myrrh
of this one temple
lingering in the air instinctively,
perfuming the air as pieces of reason,
while outside hands, were burning this city of ours,
burning like Troy.

but it was once in Uruguay
that somebody discovered the might of the hands
a voice that could not be shut
a taste of jazz and candombe in the gulp of air
that had the merit of a lit torch.

i belong to these times.
made in Uruguay
in times of collateral damage,
missing bodies, exile and torture,
and ideals to sate the thirst
and end the hunger.

i set free my avalanche of words:
i see a phosphorus doing funny faces
gestures of light
mocking the *status quo*
hands of urgent justice
trance transitioning
because these eager hands
are more
than enough.

your habit of untying my ankles

that i was made
made in Uruguay,
i knew.
and that i was walking
until i was red and one with my surroundings,
i also knew.

you seized my body
held me from my ankles
in this your habit of untying me of me
in order to make me return to walk
walk more *to be* your surroundings,
holding back my throat
ordering me not to cry.

i did not surrender
not even *to me* at every moment.
you saw my mouth bleeding
and you invited me to think
that i have bitten a plum.
but i knew that my mouth was like phosphorus light
tenuous but rather in redemption,
full of non-silences,
and in each one of my spoken silences
you chose me
to ignite me in phosphorus.

i survived your witchcraft
so i walked myself out,
for export from Uruguay.

your language opens the mouth of me

my purpose of using this white page
allowing not the ink to dry in its well
or to unravel a riddle with a stroke of a paintbrush
to leave not on this canvas,
a model of still life, *naturaleza muerta*
painted as poems without ink.

in spite, your dermis discovers the world
invites you to go beyond this canvas, ignoring my wish.
it opens you to life like blooming flowers,
fragile, tender, naïve,
possibly and effortlessly threaten,
and i night-watch
voyeur of your voyage:

so he comes to her
and opens her mouth with his tongue
with his lyric language

she is diluted in his embraces
deluded
allured into his pleasure
lurking for a kiss,
more tongue opening her mouth,
more skin standing on the tip of its own pores
pouring those vowels nasally and throaty,
sighs with sounds,
as his tongue speaks and licks
and sings in bliss.

as i watch
i think that i can replicate this new language
fill in the blank papyrus, with a eulogy
an imitation of these lovers' song
and write their pleasure away
as if their fingers yielded into my ink.

i barricade my senses
but their sensuality is heir of their night
and it opens in me a utopia
an illusion that leaves me with insomnia
instead,
a sleepwalking ghost of aimless shadow
of eyes masked with mascara,
a trickster raccoon stealing
nothing by its own weeping loneliness.

and then i return
return to your motionless image
without solving the enigma
without resolving not even a verse.

Books Available from Gival Press
Poetry

Adamah: Poème by Céline Zins; translation by Peter Schulman
    ISBN 13: 978-1-928589-46-4, $15.00
    This bilingual (French/English) collection by an eminent French poet/writer
    is adeptly translated in this premiere edition.

Bones Washed With Wine: Flint Shards from Sussex and Bliss
by Jeff Mann
    ISBN 13: 978-1-928589-14-3, $15.00
    Includes the 1999 Gival Press Poetry Award winning collection. Jeff Mann is
    "a poet to treasure both for the wealth of his language and the generosity of
    his spirit."
    — Edward Falco, author of *Acid*

Canciones para sola cuerda / Songs for a Single String
by Jesús Gardea; English translation by Robert L. Giron
    ISBN 13: 978-1-928589-09-9, $15.00
    Finalist for the 2003 Violet Crown Book Award—Literary Prose & Poetry.
    Love poems, with echoes of Neruda à la Mexicana, Gardea writes about the
    primeval quest for the perfect woman.

Dervish by Gerard Wozek
    ISBN 13: 978-1-928589-11-2, $15.00
    Winner of the 2000 Gival Press Poetry Award / Finalist for the 2002 Violet
    Crown Book Award—Literary Prose & Poetry.
    "By jove, these poems shimmer."
    —Gerry Gomez Pearlberg, author of *Mr. Bluebird*

The Great Canopy by Paula Goldman
    ISBN 13: 1-928589-31-0, $15.00
    Winner of the 2004 Gival Press Poetry Award / 2006 Independent Publisher
    Book Award—Honorable Mention for Poetry
    "Under this canopy we experience the physicality of the body through
    Goldman's wonderfully muscular verse as well the analytics of a mind that
    tackles the meaning of Orpheus or the notion of desire."
    — Richard Jackson, author of *Half Lives*

Honey by Richard Carr
ISBN 13: 978-1-928589-45-7, $15.00
Winner of the Gival Press Poetry Award
"*Honey* is a tour de force. Comprised of 100 electrifying microsonnets . . . The
whole sequence creates a narrative that becomes, like the Hapax Legomenon,
a form that occurs only once in a literature."
—Barbara Louise Ungar, author of *The Origin of the Milky Way*

Let Orpheus Take Your Hand by George Klawitter
ISBN 13: 978-1-928589-16-7, $15.00
Winner of the 2001 Gival Press Poetry Award
A thought provoking work that mixes the spiritual with stealthy desire, with
Orpheus leading us out of the pit.

Metamorphosis of the Serpent God by Robert L. Giron
ISBN 13: 978-1-928589-07-5, $12.00
This collection "...embraces the past and the present, ethnic and sexual
identity, themes both mythical and personal."
—*The Midwest Book Review*

Museum of False Starts by Chip Livingston
ISBN 13: 978-1-928589-49-5, $15.00
Livingston - a "mixed blood" poet - presents a new approach to poetry
through his experience.
"...Chip Livingston makes the ordinary exotic, erotic and extraordinary."—Ai

On the Altar of Greece by Donna J. Gelagotis Lee
ISBN 13: 978-1-92-8589-36-5, $15.00
Winner of the 2005 Gival Press Poetry Award / 2007 Eric Hoffer Book
Award: Notable for Art Category
"...*On the Altar of Greece* is like a good travel guide: it transforms reader into
visitor and nearly into resident. It takes the visitor to the authentic places that
few tourists find, places delightful yet still surprising, safe yet unexpected...."
—by Simmons B. Buntin, editor of *Terrain.org* Blog

On the Tongue by Jeff Mann
ISBN 13: 978-1-928589-35-8, $15.00
"...These poems are ...nothing short of extraordinary."
—Trebor Healey, author of *Sweet Son of Pan*

The Nature Sonnets by Jill Williams
ISBN 13: 978-1-928589-10-5, $8.95
An innovative collection of sonnets that speaks to the cycle of nature and life,
crafted with wit and clarity. "Refreshing and pleasing."
— Miles David Moore, author of *The Bears of Paris*

The Origin of the Milky Way by Barbara Louise Ungar
ISBN 13: 978-1-928589-39-6, $15.00
Winner of the 2006 Gival Press Poetry Award
"…a fearless, unflinching collection about birth and motherhood, the transformation of bodies. Ungar's poems are honestly brutal, candidly tender. Their primal immediacy and intense intimacy are realized through her dazzling sense of craft. Ungar delivers a wonderful, sensuous, visceral poetry."
—Denise Duhamel

Poetic Voices Without Borders edited by Robert L. Giron
ISBN 13: 978-1-928589-30-3, $20.00
2006 Writer's Notes Magazine Book Award—Notable for Art / 2006 Independent Publisher Book Award—Honorable Mention for Anthology An international anthology of poetry in English, French, and Spanish, including work by Grace Cavalieri, Jewell Gomez, Joy Harjo, Peter Klappert, Jaime Manrique, C.M. Mayo, E. Ethelbert Miller, Richard Peabody, Myra Sklarew and many others.

Poetic Voices Without Borders 2, edited by Robert L. Giron
ISBN 13: 978-1-928589-43-3, $20.00
Honorable Mention for Poetry—2009 San Francisco Book Festival. Featuring poets Grace Cavalieri, Rita Dove, Dana Gioia, Joy Harjo, Peter Klappert, Philip Levine, Gloria Vando, and many other fine poets in English, French, and Spanish.

Prosody in England and Elsewhere:
A Comparative Approach by Leonardo Malcovati
ISBN 13: 978-1-928589-26-6, $20.00
The perfect tool for the poet but written for a non-specialist audience.

Protection by Gregg Shapiro
ISBN 13: 978-1-928589-41-9, $15.00
"Gregg Shapiro's stunning debut marks the arrival of a new master poet on the scene. His work blows me away."
—Greg Herren, author of *Mardi Gras Mambo*

Songs for the Spirit by Robert L. Giron
ISBN 13: 978-1-928589-0802, $16.95
A psalter for the reader who is not religious but who is spiritually inclined.
"This is an extraordinary book."
—John Shelby Spong

Sweet to Burn by Beverly Burch
ISBN 13: 978-1-928589-23-5, $15.00
Winner of the 2004 Lambda Literary Award for Lesbian Poetry / Winner of the 2003 Gival Press Poetry Award — "Novelistic in scope, but packing the emotional intensity of lyric poetry..."
— Eloise Klein Healy, author of *Passing*

Tickets to a Closing Play by Janet I. Buck
ISBN 13: 978-1-928589-25-9, $15.00
Winner of the 2002 Gival Press Poetry Award
"...this rich and vibrant collection of poetry [is] not only serious and insightful, but a sheer delight to read."—Jane Butkin Roth, editor of *We Used to Be Wives: Divorce Unveiled Through Poetry*

Voyeur by Rich Murphy
ISBN 13: 978-1-928589-48-8, $15.00
Winner of the 2008 Gival Press Poetry Award
"*Voyeur* is a work of vision and virtuosity. Concerned with relationships, marriage, sex and power, the poetry is dense, rapid, dazzling, the voice commanding, the speaker charismatic...spectacular."—Richard Carr

Where a Poet Ought Not / Où c'qui faut pas by G. Tod Slone
(in English and French)
ISBN 13: 978-1-928589-42-6, $15.00
Poems inspired by French poets Léo Ferré and François Villon and the Québec poet Raymond Lévesque in what Slone characterizes as a need to speak up. "In other words, a poet should speak the truth as he sees it and fight his damnedest to overcome all the forces encouraging not to."

For a list of poetry published by Gival Press, please visit: *www.givalpress.com.*

Books available via BookMasters, Ingram, the Internet, and other outlets.

Or Write:
Gival Press, LLC
PO Box 3812
Arlington, VA 22203
703.351.0079